FANTASTIC FACTS ABOUT

INSECTS, AMPHIBIANS AND REPTILES

Author
Martin Walters

Editor
Steve Parker

Design
Pentacor

Image Co-ordination
Ian Paulyn

Production Assistant
Rachel Jones

Index
Janet de Saulles

Editorial Director
Paula Borton

Design Director
Clare Sleven

Publishing Director
Jim Miles

This is a Parragon Book
First published in 2000

Parragon, Queen Street House, 4 Queen Street, Bath, BA1 1HE, UK

Copyright © Parragon 2000

Parragon has previously printed this material in 1999 as part of the Factfinder series

2 4 6 8 10 9 7 5 3 1

Produced by Miles Kelly Publishing Ltd
Bardfield Centre, Great Bardfield, Essex CM7 4SL

All rights reserved. No part of this publication may be reproduced,
stored in a retrieval system, or transmitted by any means, electronic, mechanical,
photocopying, recording or otherwise, without the prior permission of the copyright holder.

ISBN 0-75253-388-6

Printed in Italy Milanostampa Caleppio Milano

FANTASTIC FACTS ABOUT

INSECTS, AMPHIBIANS AND REPTILES

p

Contents

Introduction 6

INVERTEBRATE ANIMALS 8
Tiny and Simple Animals 10
Jellyfish and Anemones 12
Worms 14
More Worms 16
Molluscs 18
Starfish and Urchins 20
Butterflies 22
Flies, Bees and Wasps 24
Beetles and Bugs 26
Dragonflies 28
Grasshoppers 30
Spiders and Mites 32
Spiders and Scorpions 34
Crabs and Prawns 36
Small Crustaceans 38

AMPHIBIANS 40
Frogs and Toads 42
Salamanders and Newts 44

REPTILES 46
Turtles 48
Tortoises 50
Big Lizards 52
Smaller Lizards 54
Non-poisonous Snakes 56
Poisonous Snakes 58
Crocodiles 60

Index 62
Acknowledgements 64

INTRODUCTION

Creepy-crawly insects and spine-chilling reptiles are probably some of the most fascinating creatures in the animal kingdom. Here you will find bugs, beetles, butterflies and spiders along with many other invertebrates. You will encounter poisonous frogs, spitting cobras, deadly black mambas, slow-moving turtles, skinks with blue tongues and snapping crocodiles. And you will also discover many creatures you never even knew existed!

INSECTS AND REPTILES is a handy reference guide in the *Fascinating Facts* series. Each book has been specially compiled with a collection of stunning illustrations and photographs which bring the subject to life. Hundreds of facts and figures are presented in a variety of interesting ways and side-panels provide information at-a-glance. This unique combination is fun and easy to use and makes learning a pleasure.

INTRODUCTION TO

INVERTEBRATE ANIMALS

The invertebrates are those animals which have no backbone (vertebral column). In fact, most animals are invertebrates – in all, about 98 out of every 100 of living species. Although they are so numerous, many invertebrates are small, and not as conspicuous as their bigger cousins the vertebrates – the animals with backbones.

The largest main group, or phylum, within the invertebrates is the arthropods. (The name means 'jointed-limbed'.) This phylum includes the insects (the biggest of any single animal group), the spiders and other arachnids, and the crustaceans, which include crabs, prawns and shrimps.

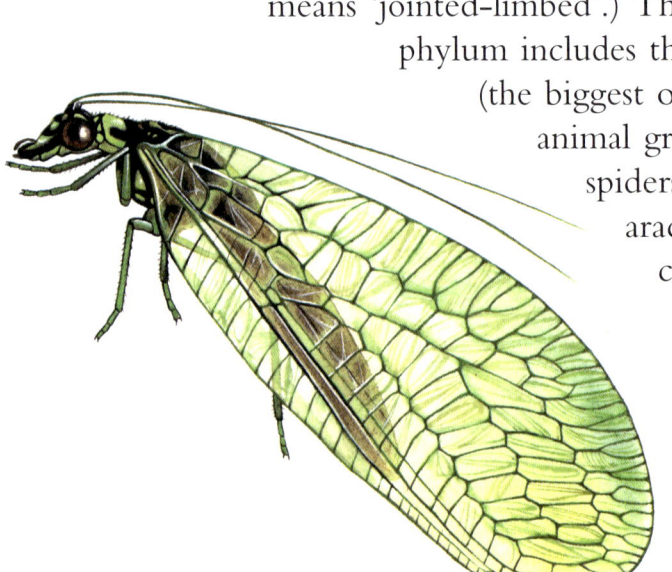

SOFT OR HARD BODIES?
Some invertebrates, such as jellyfish and worms, have very soft bodies. Others, however, notably the arthropods, have tough, rigid bodies with a shell-like outer skeleton. Many molluscs, such as snails, produce a hard chalky shell to protect the soft body within.

INVERTEBRATE ANIMALS

TINY AND SIMPLE ANIMALS

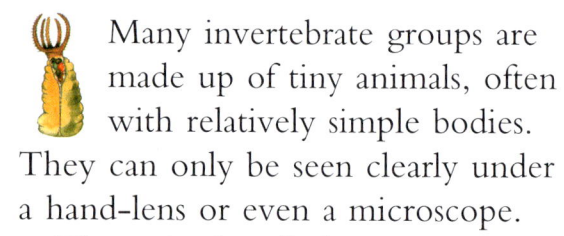

Many invertebrate groups are made up of tiny animals, often with relatively simple bodies. They can only be seen clearly under a hand-lens or even a microscope.

The animals called sponges can be large, but their individual cells are very simple. Indeed, sponges look more like plants than animals. Adult sponges cannot move about, although they do twitch slightly at the surface when touched. They catch their food – even tinier plants and animals – by filtering it out of the water. They also obtain dissolved oxygen in the same way.

Water-bears (their scientific name is tardigrades, meaning 'slow-moving') are amazing microscopic creatures, with powers as strange as their

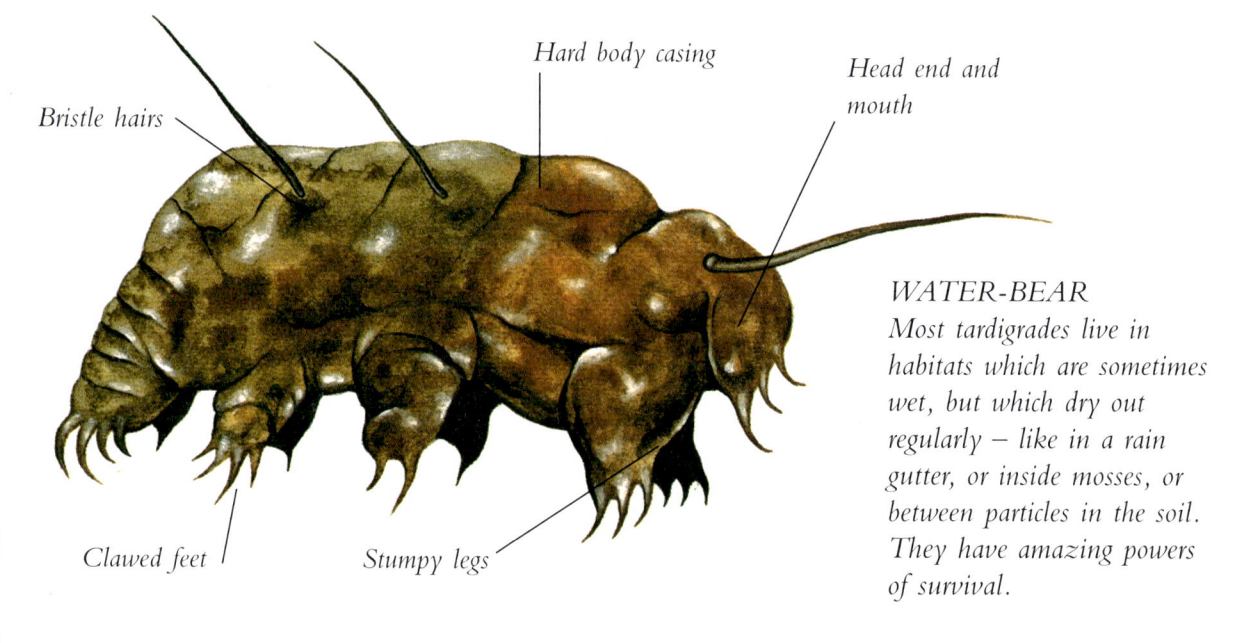

Hard body casing

Head end and mouth

Bristle hairs

Clawed feet

Stumpy legs

WATER-BEAR
Most tardigrades live in habitats which are sometimes wet, but which dry out regularly – like in a rain gutter, or inside mosses, or between particles in the soil. They have amazing powers of survival.

appearance. They look like tiny bears, with their plump bodies and stumpy, clawed legs. They are very small, ranging from 0.05 millimetres to just over one millimetre in length.

Food being digested

jelly-like body casing

ROTIFER
Rotifers or 'wheel-animacules' take their name from the special rings of hair-like structures called cilia on their heads, which look a bit like wheels.

SPONGE
Sponges grow in many shapes, such as cups, tall columns and flat plates. Most live in the sea but a few dwell in fresh water.

Sponges
10,000 species
- many have spiky skeletons
- adults live fixed to bottom of sea
- body full of holes

Water-bears
400 species
- microscopic
- four pairs of stumpy legs, with bristly claws
- most live in damp places; some in fresh water; a few marine

Wheel-animacules
1,800 species
- microscopic
- crown of cilia (wheel-like in some)
- live in fresh water; some marine; some in damp places

Moss animals
4,000 species
- aquatic; mostly marine
- each animal has a bell-shaped ring of tentacles

INVERTEBRATE ANIMALS

JELLYFISH AND ANEMONES

This group, the cnidarians or coelenterates, includes the corals and sea anemones as well as all the various kinds of jellyfish. Nearly all these animals live in the sea, and most have circular bodies with a ring of tentacles. Many have barbed cells, which can give a nasty sting! A few are so venomous that they can actually kill people.

Many jellyfish, sea anemones and corals are beautifully coloured, often in shades of pink, red, yellow and orange. Most have very soft, rather squashy bodies made up of two layers of cells surrounding a jelly-like substance. Some, like the corals, build themselves hard,stony, external skeletons to protect their soft bodies from attack. These external skeletons build up in their millions to form the rocks of a coral reef.

Bell (main body)

JELLYFISH
Moon jellyfish (Aurelia aurita) grow to about 40 centimetres across. Some jellyfish can swim weakly using pulsating movements of the main body or bell. Most catch prey such as small fish, shrimps, prawns and worms.

Stinging tentacles capture prey

12

MAN-O-WAR
This is actually a colony of small individual jellyfish-like creatures. Its gas-filled float catches the breeze and moves it along, rather like a sailing ship. Its stinging tentacles may be 30 metres long.

FRESHWATER TYPES

A few members of the cnidarian group live in fresh water. An example is the hydra. It looks a bit like a miniature sea anemone, with a long stalk and waving tentacles.

COMB-JELLY
The comb-jellies or ctenophores are similar to jellyfish. They live in the sea and catch tiny animals and plants for food. They also glow at night, making the sea light up with an eerie greenish sheen.

Jellyfish and relatives (Cnidaria/Coelenterata)
10,000 species
- mostly marine, some freshwater
- circular body plan
- mouth surrounded by tentacles
- soft-bodied, but some (like certain corals) make hard outer skeletons

Two main subgroups:

Anemones and corals
6,000 species
- marine
- adults attached to a hard surface
- flower-like body shape

Jellyfish and hydroids
4,000 species
- most marine; a few freshwater
- adults either free-swimming or attached
- some live as colonies
- many have dangerous stings

INVERTEBRATE ANIMALS

WORMS

True worms have tube-shaped bodies, divided up into segments or rings. Earthworms are a common kind of segmented worm and are familiar garden creatures. They live in most kinds of soil, especially in old meadows and under grassy lawns. Earthworms have short bristles on their bodies which help them to grip the soil when they are burrowing. An earthworm has no obvious head – the front and tail end look similar, except the head is slightly more pointed.

Most segmented worms live in the sea. These are the bristleworms, which include the familiar lugworms found in seaside sand, and many different kinds of ragworm. Some bristleworms can swim about in the sea, but most of them make burrows or tubes in the sand or mud.

Head with jaw-like mouthparts

Parapodia along sides of body

RAGWORM
The flap-like parts along the ragworm's body are called parapodia. They work as gills to absorb oxygen from the water, and as paddles when swimming. The ragworm is a fierce seashore predator and can give a painful bite.

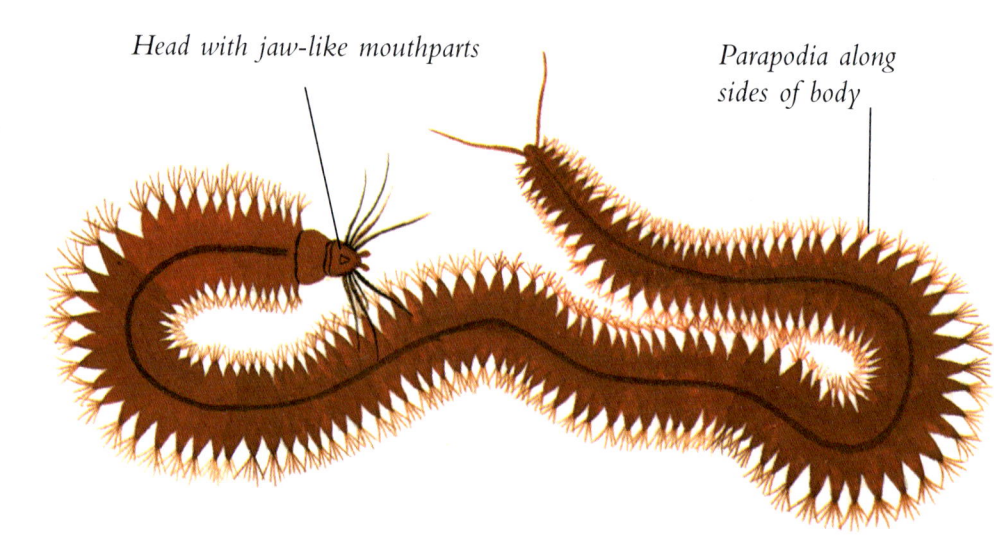

BLOOD-SUCKERS

Another group of worms, this time mainly freshwater, are the leeches. Leeches are flattened worms. They have muscular bodies which can contract or extend, and a sucker at each end.

Flattened, leaf-like body

Rear sucker

Some leeches prey on worms, molluscs or insect larvae, but many are parasites, sucking the blood of fish or other animals. Some occasionally suck blood from people.

Front sucker under head end

Body compartments or segments

LEECH
A leech can ripple or undulate its body, to swim along. On land it anchors its front sucker, shortens its body, anchors the rear sucker, extends the body, and so on.

Segmented worms
15,000 species
- tube-shaped body
- body divided into segments
- soft body

Three main subgroups:

Earthworms
4,000 species
- most live on land or in fresh water
- hermaphrodite (each individual is both male and female)

Leeches
500 species
- freshwater; some marine or land-living
- some suck blood
- hermaphrodite

Bristleworms
10,500 species
- most are marine
- body has bristles, sometimes used as paddles
- sexes separate
- includes ragworms and lugworms

INVERTEBRATE ANIMALS

MORE WORMS

Flatworms and roundworms are both common types of worm. Flatworms have bodies which are flattened in outline, almost like a normal worm which has been ironed out. Many are very small, and some live as parasites inside other animals. They show no segments, although some of the parasitic forms have divisions along their bodies.

ROUNDWORMS
About 20,000 different kinds of roundworm or nematode worm have been discovered, but the true number may be nearer to 500,000! Roundworms inhabit just about every habitat, especially soil. But even though they are so common, most of them are very small, only a few millimetres long. So we do not see them as often as larger worms such as earthworms.

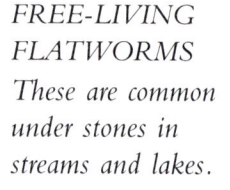

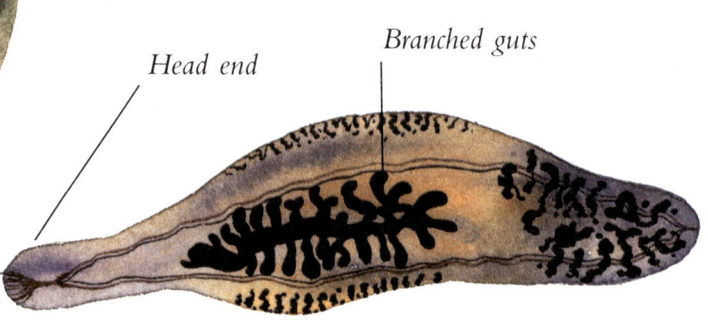

FREE-LIVING FLATWORMS
These are common under stones in streams and lakes.

Head end

Branched guts

LIVER FLUKE
This flatworm is a parasite, burrowing into the liver.

16

ROUNDWORM
The pig nematode worm, Ascaris, lives in the guts and flesh of pigs and similar animals. If pork meat is not cooked properly, this parasite can pass into the human body as tiny eggs, and then grow and cause an infestation. This is why it is important to cook pork meat thoroughly, to kill any roundworm eggs.

Head end

TAPEWORMS
These worms have long, ribbon-like bodies – up to 10 metres! Most live as parasites inside the intestines of larger animals, including people. At the front end, the tapeworm secures itself to the gut wall of its host with hooks and suckers.

Proglottis

TAPEWORM
Each section of the body is not a segment, but a separate bag or 'proglottis' full of reproductive parts and eggs.

Flatworms
25,000 species
- live in water or damp places, or inside other animals
- soft, flattened body
- no segments
- most are hermaphrodite
- some are free-living, some are parasites
- divided into three groups, the free-living flatworms (Turbellaria), flukes (Trematoda) and tapeworms (Cestoda)

Roundworms
20,000 species
- found in all habitats
- most are free-living; some are parasites
- body rounded, but without segments

Ribbon worms
900 species
- most are marine
- long and ribbon-shaped
- catch and eat other animals

17

INVERTEBRATE ANIMALS

MOLLUSCS

Molluscs are one of the most varied of all the animal groups, containing creatures as different as octopuses, squids, snails, slugs and shellfish such as oysters and mussels. There are nearly 100,000 species, making them the second largest of all the animal groups, after the arthropods. Even though some molluscs have hard shells, they all have soft bodies. Unlike the arthropods, molluscs do not have jointed limbs. Instead, most molluscs move about on a large flat pad, or foot. The head of a mollusc often has soft tentacles, used to feel the way.

MOSTLY MARINE
Most molluscs live in the sea, with only two groups, the bivalves and the snails, having some species which live in fresh water. Some snails have even adapted very well to life on dry land, although they are active only in damp conditions.

GARDEN SNAIL
Snails and slugs, including the sea-snails and sea-slugs, and the limpets, belong to a group of molluscs known as gastropods, meaning 'stomach-foot'. This is because they seem to walk or crawl along on their bellies.

Fleshy body-covering or mantle

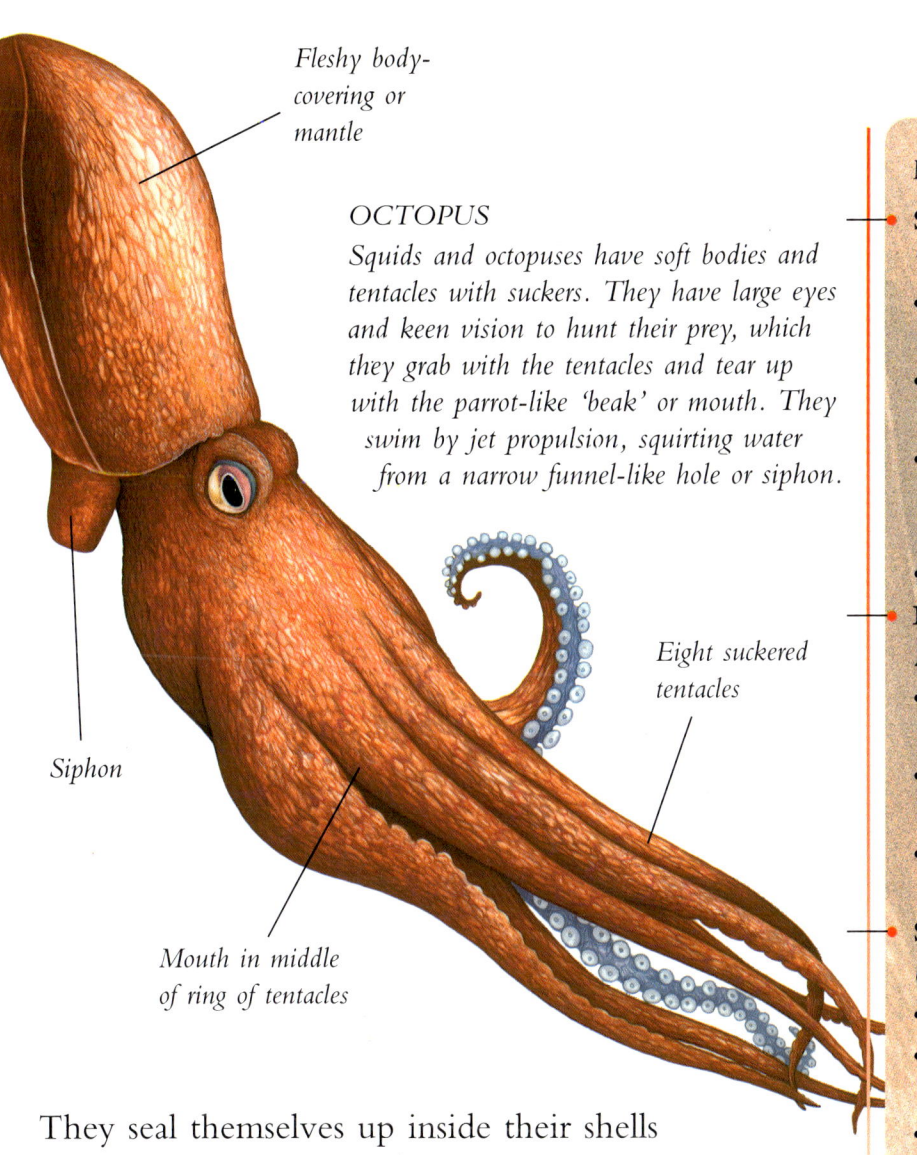

OCTOPUS

Squids and octopuses have soft bodies and tentacles with suckers. They have large eyes and keen vision to hunt their prey, which they grab with the tentacles and tear up with the parrot-like 'beak' or mouth. They swim by jet propulsion, squirting water from a narrow funnel-like hole or siphon.

Siphon

Eight suckered tentacles

Mouth in middle of ring of tentacles

They seal themselves up inside their shells if the weather gets too dry.

The mollusc group includes the largest of all invertebrates, the giant squid, and also some of the most 'intelligent' invertebrates, octopuses and cuttlefish.

Main subgroups of molluscs:

- **Slugs and snails**

  77,000 species
  - marine, freshwater and land-living
  - most have a single shell, often coiled
  - head has tentacles, sometimes tipped by simple eyes
  - walk on muscular foot

- **Bivalves**

  20,000 species
  - most are marine, some freshwater
  - hinged shell of two parts (or valves)
  - most burrow, or live attached to rocks

- **Squids and octopuses**

  650 species
  - marine
  - tentacles surround the mouth
  - large eyes
  - hide among rocks or swim in the sea

INVERTEBRATE ANIMALS

STARFISH AND URCHINS

Starfish belong to a group called the echinoderms, which means 'prickly skin', and many of them are indeed rough-skinned or spiny. As well as starfish, the echinoderms include feather-stars and sea-lilies, brittlestars, sea urchins and sand dollars, and sea cucumbers. All echinoderms live in the sea.

HOW MANY ARMS?
Starfish have arms which spread out from the centre, in a star-like pattern. Many kinds of starfish have five arms, though some have seven, and others as many as 14. Underneath each arm there are rows of small flexible tube-shaped feet, which the starfish uses to creep slowly about, or to prise open shellfish to eat.

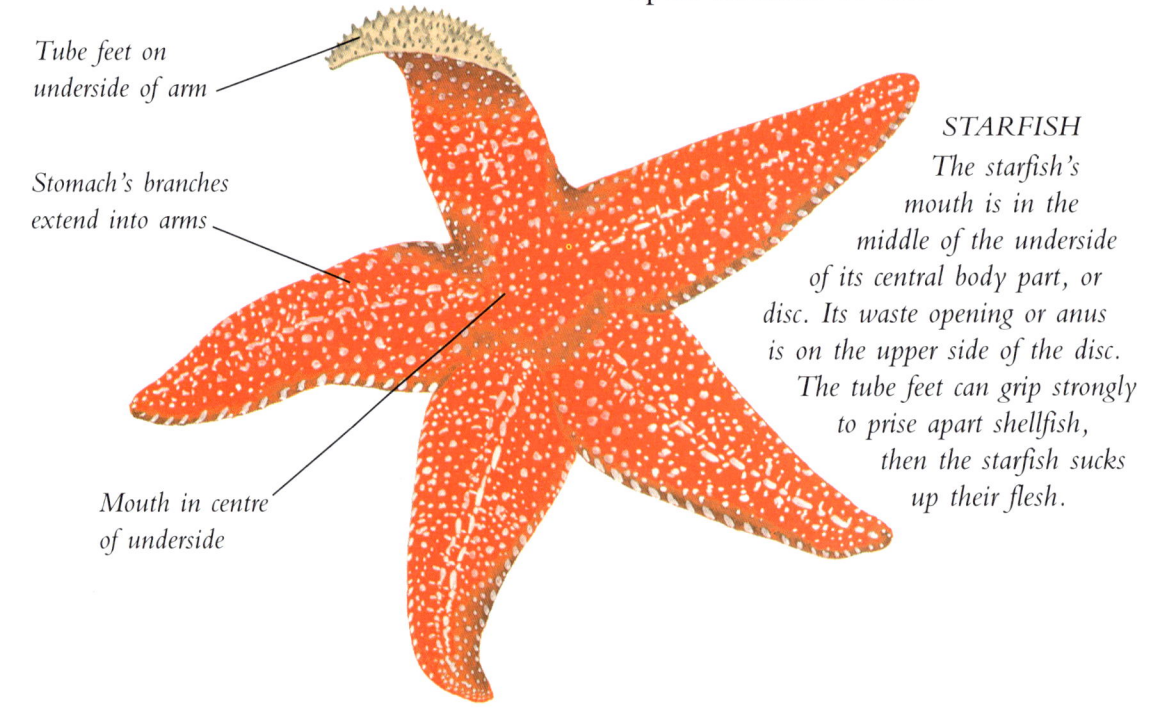

Tube feet on underside of arm

Stomach's branches extend into arms

Mouth in centre of underside

STARFISH
The starfish's mouth is in the middle of the underside of its central body part, or disc. Its waste opening or anus is on the upper side of the disc. The tube feet can grip strongly to prise apart shellfish, then the starfish sucks up their flesh.

Sea urchins and sand dollars have rounded bodies, either ball-shaped, or flattened, and many have long spines. They also have a five-part radial body plan, but since they do not have arms, this plan is much less obvious than in starfish. They use their spines to lever themselves along slowly, and can also climb by using their tube-feet. Sea urchins feed by scraping the thin layer of tiny plants and animals, such as corals, off rocks.

Arms around head

Sausage-shaped body

SEA CUCUMBER
Some sea cucumbers live in shallow water near the shore. But they are far more common at great depths on the ocean floor. They crawl along slowly, sieving the mud and sand for tiny edible particles. In some places, people consider that the sex organs (gonads) of sea cucumbers are a great delicacy to eat.

Subgroups of echinoderms:

Starfish
1,500 species
- flat and star-shaped
- usually 5 arms (some have more)

Brittle-stars
2,000 species
- flat and star-shaped
- usually 5 arms, which are long and brittle

Feather stars and sea-lilies
625 species
- either swimming (feather stars) or stalked (sea-lilies)
- feed by filtering sea water

Sea urchins
950 species
- body rounded, often hard with long spines
- no arms

Sea cucumbers
1,150 species
- body long and tube-shaped
- tentacles around mouth

INVERTEBRATE ANIMALS

BUTTERFLIES

Insects have jointed limbs and bodies which are clearly divided into three main sections – the head, thorax (chest) and abdomen. Most adult insects have three pairs of legs, attached to the thorax. Many adult insects also have one or two pairs of wings, also attached to the thorax.

Butterflies and moths, with about 175,000 species, make up the second largest group of insects, after the beetles. They can be found wherever there are trees and flowers, but are most numerous in tropical and warmer parts of the world. Most species have four large, rather papery and delicate wings, often brightly patterned and coloured, covered with tiny scales.

BUTTERFLY COLOURS
The bright colours of the zebra butterfly advertise its presence to potential mates at breeding time.

BUTTERFLY OR MOTH?
Most butterflies, like this tropical blue, have clubbed antennae, fly by day, hold their wings out sideways at rest, and are colourful. Most moths have feathery antennae, fly at night, hold their wings together at rest, and have drab colours.

Stage 1: Egg

Stage 2: Caterpillar or larva

Stage 3: Chrysalis or pupa

Stage 4: Adult or imago

INSECT LIFE CYCLE

Some insects, such as butterflies and beetles, have a four-stage life cycle (shown above for the brimstone butterfly). They change body shape from one stage to the next, a process known as metamorphosis.

Insects

At least one million species, perhaps ten times that number
- body divided into three main parts – head, thorax, abdomen
- three pairs of legs, in adult and perhaps also immature stages
- most have two pairs of wings, although true flies have one pair
- most are land-living or in fresh water (there are hardly any insects in the sea)

The following pages cover the main subgroups of insects:

Butterflies and moths

175,000 species
- adults have two pairs of wings, often colourful
- adult has long tube-like tongue
- larvae are caterpillars and eat leaves
- most adults feed on nectar from flowers

23

INVERTEBRATE ANIMALS

FLIES, BEES AND WASPS

The true flies form a group of more than 90,000 species worldwide. They include houseflies, gnats and midges, craneflies, horseflies, hoverflies, fruitflies, bluebottles and dungflies. The main feature of the true flies is that they have just one main pair of wings. The second (hind) pair of wings have become thin and club-shaped, used to help the fly balance in flight.

MOSQUITO
This tiny type of fly is a blood-sucker. It uses its sharp, needle-like mouthparts to drill a tiny hole into the skin, and sucks up blood from its victim. Usually only the female does this, to get nutrients for making her eggs.

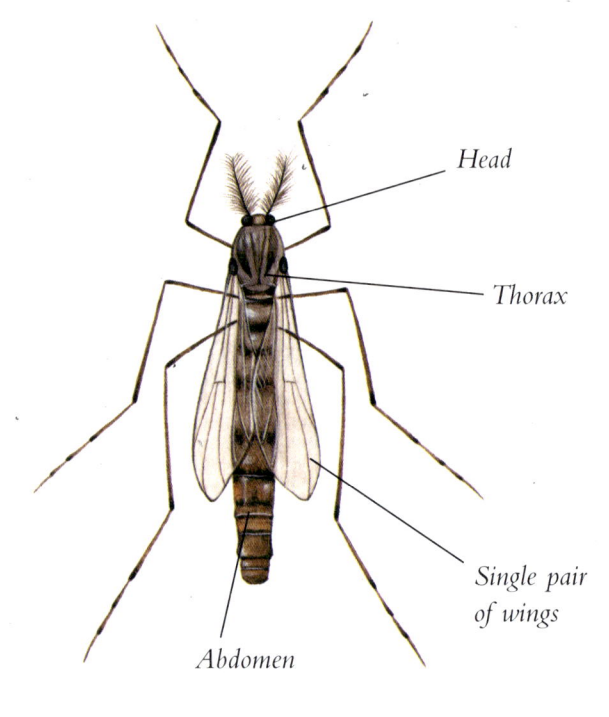

Head
Thorax
Single pair of wings
Abdomen

MIDGE
Gnats and midges are among the smallest insects. Some feed on flowers or plants. Others are blood-suckers, although few have mouthparts strong enough to pierce human skin.

SOCIAL INSECTS

The insect group Hymenoptera includes the familiar honeybees, bumblebees, wasps and ants, and also over 100,000 species of parasitic wasps. These are less well known, and many of them are very small.

Some members of this group are social, living together with their own kind in colonies. The members help with different tasks, such as fetching and delivering food, cleaning, and defending the nest from attack. Some ants, called driver ants and army ants, march along in columns when they search for food, and there may be over 500,000 ants all moving along together.

COMMON WASP
Most wasps have a venomous sting at the rear of the abdomen. They can use this several times, unlike the bee, which can only sting once and then dies.

Further subgroups of insects:

Flies
90,000 species
- one pair of transparent wings
- second pair of wings are tiny club-shaped halteres, which work like gyroscopes to give better balance in flight
- larvae are legless grubs or maggots

Bees, wasps and ants
130,000 species
- two pairs of thin wings, the front and rear of each side joined together
- chewing mouthparts
- ants are mainly wingless
- many can sting
- many feed from flowers
- the main types of social insects, along with termites (a different group)

BEETLES AND BUGS

The largest group of insects are the beetles, with over 400,000 species. In most beetles, the first pair of wings are hard and form a protective case for the wings and body when the insect is at rest. When a beetle flies, it first has to unfurl its thin wings from underneath its hard wing cases. You may have seen a ladybird folding up its wings again just after landing, and tucking them back inside its wing covers.

Weevils form the largest family of beetles, with more than 60,000 species. They feed on plants – often on the seeds, fruits and flowers. Weevils have a long, curved snout.

LOUSE
Lice are mostly parasites, sucking the blood or body fluids of mammals, birds and other larger creatures. The louse's legs are shaped like hooks, to cling tightly to the host's skin or hair.

SINGING CICADAS
Cicadas are large, tree-living bugs. The cicada's song is not really a song at all, and comes not from its mouthparts but from the sides of its body. The cicada vibrates a special drum-like part of its hard skin or cuticle, flicking it in and out rather like a tin lid, only much more rapidly, making a really loud sizzling or fizzing sound. It usually does this to attract a mate.

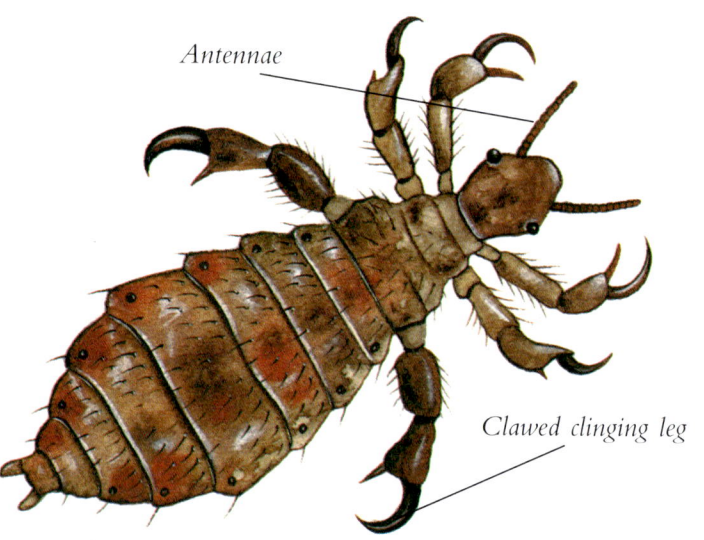

Antennae

Clawed clinging leg

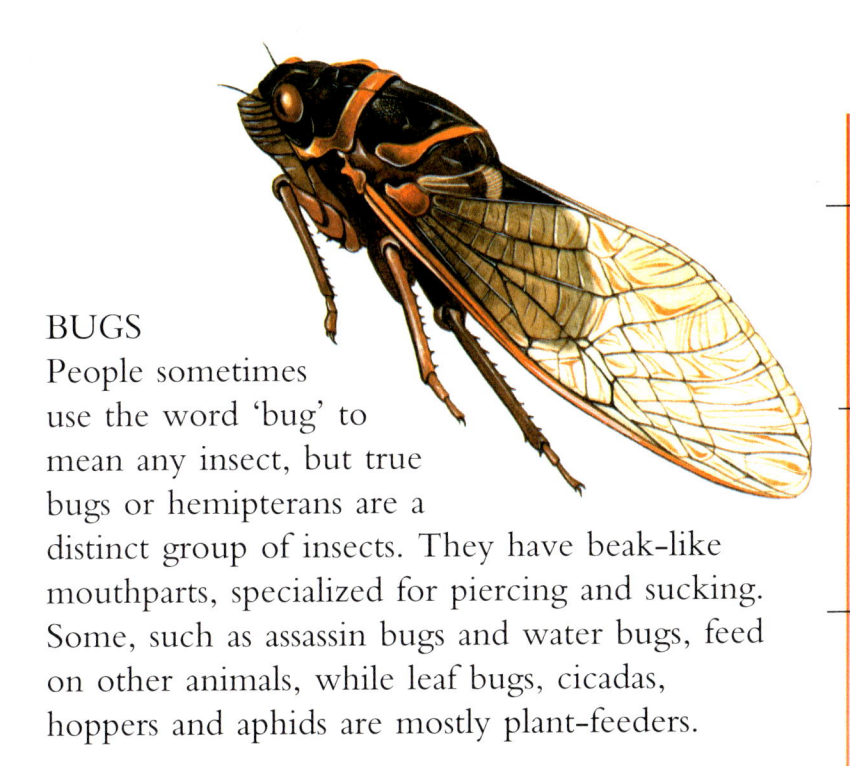

BUGS
People sometimes use the word 'bug' to mean any insect, but true bugs or hemipterans are a distinct group of insects. They have beak-like mouthparts, specialized for piercing and sucking. Some, such as assassin bugs and water bugs, feed on other animals, while leaf bugs, cicadas, hoppers and aphids are mostly plant-feeders.

*LACEWING
The lacewings are hunters of smaller creatures such as aphids (greenfly and blackfly), members of the bug group.*

Further subgroups of insects:

Beetles and weevils
400,000 species
- front wings are hard wing-cases
- biting mouthparts

True bugs
70,000 species
- mouthparts for piercing and sucking
- many have flattened bodies

Lice
3,200 species
- most are parasites on warm-blooded animals
- lack wings
- sucking mouthparts
- hook-like legs for clinging

Lacewings and ant-lions
5,000 species
- lace-like veins in the wings
- larvae catch and eat other insects
- mainly in warm countries

27

INVERTEBRATE ANIMALS

DRAGONFLIES

Dragonflies are some of the most impressive of all insects with their shiny colours and masterful, rapid flight. They can accelerate in seconds to speeds of more than 50 kilometres per hour, and also hover quite still. These skills allow them to catch other flying insects, such as a midge or gnat, in mid-air.

Damselflies are smaller cousins of dragonflies. Both dragonflies and damselflies live for a year or longer as larvae or nymphs in streams and rivers. They are powerful predators of smaller animals such as young fish and tadpoles.

EARWIGS
Earwigs may look quite fierce, with their curved claw-like tails, but are actually harmless. They burrow about in the garden soil where they eat a range of plant and animal food, including many harmful grubs.

IN THE WATER
The young or immature mayfly is called a nymph. It lives in fresh water for many months, shedding its skin as it grows, before crawling up a plant stem to change into an adult.

28

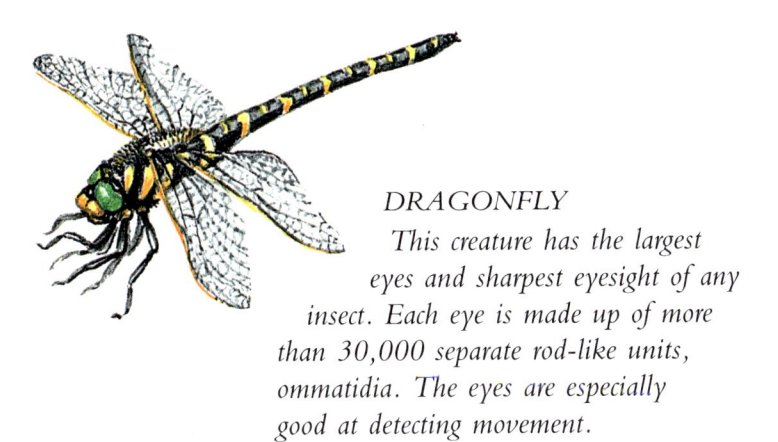

DRAGONFLY
This creature has the largest eyes and sharpest eyesight of any insect. Each eye is made up of more than 30,000 separate rod-like units, ommatidia. The eyes are especially good at detecting movement.

FAST FOOD

Mantises catch and eat other animals, such as large insects and spiders, grabbing them in a flash using their spiny front legs. Their large eyes give them the good vision needed to spot and pounce at their prey.

PRAYING MANTIS
The mantis sits patiently on a plant or flower, waiting until a suitable insect passes close enough. Then it strikes, lightning-quick, to secure its next meal.

Further subgroups of insects:

- **Dragonflies and damselflies**
  5,000 species
  - mainly large
  - two pairs of large, transparent wings
  - big eyes
  - young (nymphs) are aquatic

- **Mantises**
  1,800 species
  - triangular head, big eyes
  - large front legs with pincer-like claws
  - eat mainly other insects
  - mainly in warm countries

- **Earwigs**
  1,200 species
  - flattened body
  - pincers at tail end
  - very long, flimsy wings

INVERTEBRATE ANIMALS

GRASSHOPPERS

The main features of crickets and grasshoppers are their powerful hind legs, equipped with large muscles. These insects use their legs to make sudden leaps to escape predators. Most members of this group have camouflaged bodies, patterned to blend in with their habitat, and they are very difficult to spot until they jump or fly away.

CHIRPING FOR A MATE
A summer's day in a meadow is seldom without the background chirping sounds of crickets and grasshoppers. These insects have two different methods of 'singing'. Crickets and katydids rub the veins of their rough front wings together. Grasshoppers and locusts rub their back legs against the front wings. Each leg has a row of hard pegs which make the wing vibrate as they pass over it.

GRASSHOPPER
Most grasshoppers have short antennae, about the length of the head. Many crickets have much longer antennae, sometimes four or five times the body length. Both these types of insects eat plant food such as leaves and shoots.

Large powerful rear leg

Wings flutter open to glide down after leaping

30

ADULT MAYFLY
The adult mayfly has very small, undeveloped mouthparts. It cannot feed. It lives for less than a day, flitting over water to attract a mate. Then the male dies. The female lasts slightly longer – she lays her eggs and then dies.

A SHORT LIFE
Mayflies live for a year or longer as larvae in streams and rivers. But the adults, which often hatch out all at the same time, live for only a few hours.

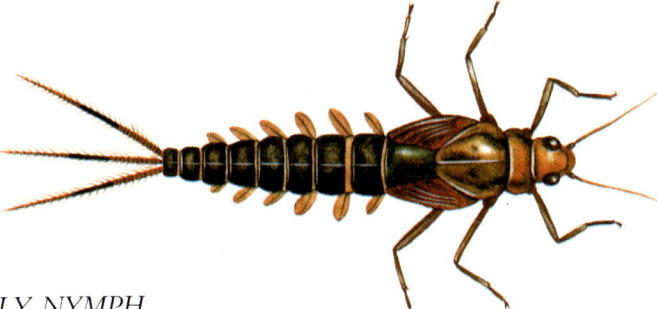

MAYFLY NYMPH
The immature mayfly crawls on the bottom of a pond or stream, feeding on old bits of plant and animal matter.

Further subgroups of insects:

Crickets and grasshoppers
20,500 species
- large hind legs for jumping
- shield-like covering behind the head
- front wings hardened as protection for rear wings

Stick and leaf insects
2,500 species
- leaf insects (mainly South East Asia and Australia) look like leaves
- stick insects (tropics worldwide) look like sticks
- mainly in warm countries
- eat various kinds of plant food

Mayflies
2,000 species
- delicate veined wings (usually two pairs)
- three tails
- young (nymphs) are aquatic
- adults very short-lived
- adults stay near fresh water

INVERTEBRATE ANIMALS

SPIDERS AND MITES

The arachnids are spiders, scorpions, ticks and mites and harvestmen. Like insects, arachnids are mostly land-living, with just a few kinds of spiders and mites living in fresh water, and one kind in the sea. With some 86,500 species they make up the second largest group of arthropods, after the insects.

Spiders have a special ability which sets them apart from most other animals. They can make a kind of silken thread. Spiders use their silk to make cocoons for their eggs, as well as for many different designs of traps and webs to catch their prey. Spider silk is one of the strongest materials known. It is stronger than steel wire of the same thickness!

MITES
These small creatures, along with ticks, are tiny eight-legged relatives of spiders.

32

BIRD-EATING SPIDER
This type of spider rarely makes a web. It runs after its prey and subdues it with a bite from the venomous fangs which all spiders possess.

TYPES OF SILK

The webs of orb-web spiders are the most complicated, with two kinds of silk. Thicker, tough thread is used for the main framework. The cross-threads are spun from a more stretchy, sticky type of silk that traps the victim.

TRAPDOOR SPIDER
This spider lives in burrows, using silk to make a covering to the entrance, with a hinged lid. It sits in its burrow and leaps out when a suitable small creature passes by. Then it drags its prey back down into the burrow.

Main subgroups of arachnids:

Spiders
50,000 species
- eight legs
- worldwide, all habitats
- body has obvious waist between head part (cephalothorax) and abdomen
- make webs from silk
- poison fangs

Harvestmen
4,500 species
- like a spider with long, stilt-like legs
- rounded one-part body

Ticks and mites
32,000 species
- most are small (mites about 1 millimetre, some ticks reach 3 centimetres)
- ticks are parasites of mammals, birds or reptiles
- some mites are parasites, others free-living
- mites are often brightly coloured

33

SPIDERS AND SCORPIONS

SUN SPIDER
Not a true spider, the sun or wind spider has its own arachnid group, the solifuges. It is extremely fierce and as it lacks poison fangs, it crushes its prey to death with its huge mouthparts.

Scorpions have long bodies and large pincers which make them look like miniature lobsters. The scorpion's secret weapon is the sting at the end of its long, arching tail. It uses this to immobilize larger prey and to defend itself. Several kinds of scorpion can inflict very painful stings. A few can even kill large mammals, including people.

OUT AT NIGHT

Scorpions are mainly active during the night. By day they hide squeezed into a crevice in a rock, or wedged under a stone or log. Scorpions can feel vibrations in the soil and this is probably how they find their prey. When a scorpion catches up with its prey it grabs the prey with its large pincers, and may then sting the prey to stop it struggling.

MOTHER SCORPION

A female scorpion may lay dozens of eggs. When these hatch, the tiny baby scorpions clamber onto their mother's back. She carries and takes care of them until they can fend for themselves.

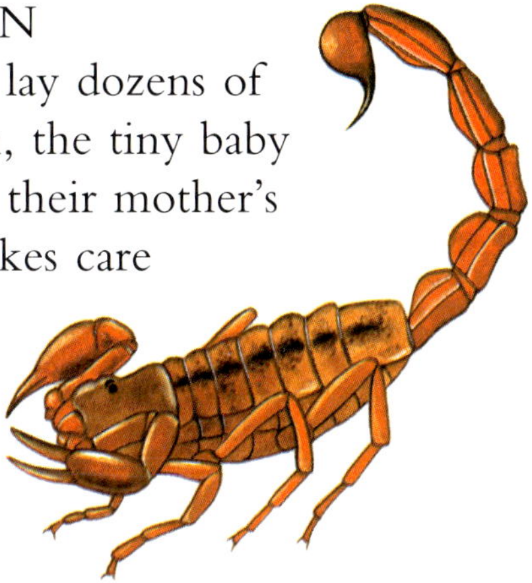

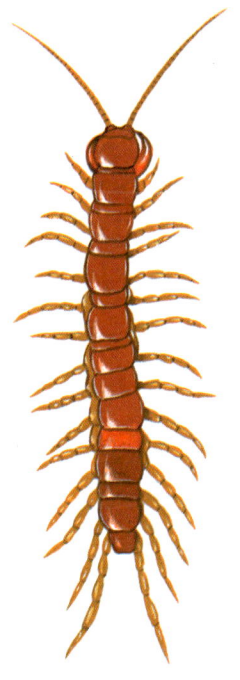

MANY LEGS

Centipedes live under logs and among leaf litter. They use their sharp jaws to catch their prey, which they inject with a poisonous bite. Most centipedes can run fast, using their many long legs, one pair per segment. Millipedes are slower moving than centipedes, have more rounded bodies with two pairs of legs per segment, and eat dead and decaying matter.

Centipede

Millipede

Another arachnid subgroup:

Scorpions
1,200 species
- worldwide, in warmer countries
- large pincers
- curved tail with poisonous sting

More groups of arthropods:

Millipedes
8,000 species
- found throughout the world
- mainly in the soil
- herbivores
- many legs
- tubular, rounded bodies
- short feelers

Centipedes
3,000 species
- worldwide
- mainly in the soil or under rocks or wood
- carnivores
- many legs, flattened bodies
- long feelers
- sharp poisonous jaws

INVERTEBRATE ANIMALS

CRABS AND PRAWNS

Insects are the commonest arthropods on land and in the air. But in the water, crustaceans are the most prominent. They include crabs, lobsters, crayfish, shrimps, prawns, barnacles and water-fleas. Most crustaceans live in the sea, but some live in fresh water, and a few, such as woodlice, even live on land, though usually close to water, or in damp habitats.

Tropical prawn

CRABS

There are thousands of kinds of crabs, from giant spider-crabs with claws spanning three metres or more, to tiny species no bigger than a pea. Crabs have very flattened bodies almost entirely protected by their hard shell-like carapace. Crabs walk on four pairs of legs and most have one pair of large curved pincers.

SHORE CRAB
This adaptable crustacean can live in salty or fresh water, and survive in air for several hours. It also eats almost any kind of food, from old seaweed to rotting fish.

SHRIMPS AND PRAWNS

These are like miniature lobsters or crayfish, but they are smaller, lighter, and swim well. They use their small pincers to pick up tiny pieces of food, and their long antennae or feelers to detect objects and also water currents.

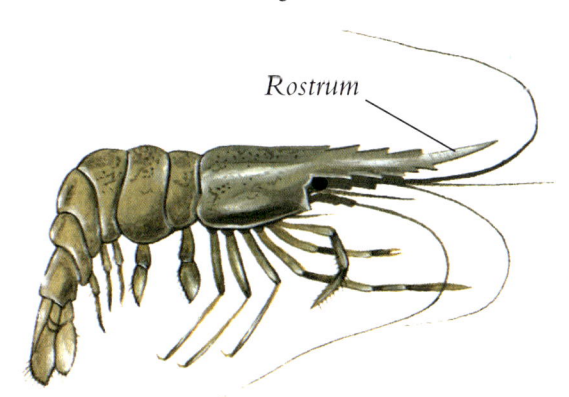

Rostrum

Prawn

SHRIMP OR PRAWN?

Shrimps and prawns are very similar to each other. The main difference is that prawns have a long, pointed extension to the carapace sticking out in front of the head, rather like a beak. This is called the rostrum.

Shrimp

Swimmerets (paddle-like swimming limbs)

Main subgroups of crustaceans:

Crabs
5,700 species
- mostly marine (some in fresh water or on land)
- flattened body, with hard shell
- crawl on seabed
- large pair of pincers
- four pairs of walking legs

Lobsters and crayfish
400 species
- mostly marine (some in fresh water or on land)
- long body
- crawl on seabed
- large pair of pincers
- four pairs of walking legs

Shrimps and prawns
2,000 species
- mainly marine
- long-bodied
- swim and crawl well
- long antennae

SMALL CRUSTACEANS

In addition to familiar prawns and crabs, the crustacean group contains several smaller, less known types of creatures. One of the most beautiful is the fairy shrimp. This looks like a water-dwelling woodlouse and moves along slowly, using wavy movements of its legs to swim. One of the oddest things about the fairy shrimp is that it swims upside-down.

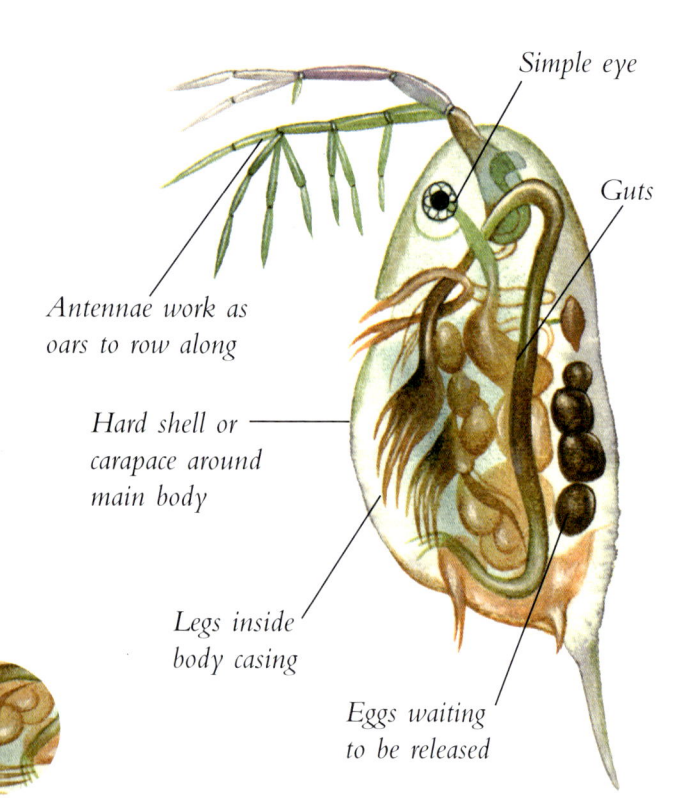

These creatures have no defences against predators, but they live in temporary pools and puddles where predatory animals, such as fish, cannot survive. When the pool dries out, the adult fairy shrimps die, but the eggs which have gathered in the mud survive until the pool fills again – perhaps years later.

Simple eye

Guts

Antennae work as oars to row along

Hard shell or carapace around main body

Legs inside body casing

Eggs waiting to be released

WATER-FLEA
Water-fleas (daphnia) have feathery antennae, and they use these to row themselves about in the water. As they move, they breathe using their limbs, which act like gills and take in oxygen from the water. If you look carefully at a water-flea you may see the eggs inside its transparent body. The eggs develop inside a special pouch called the brood chamber.

BY THE BILLION

The open seas and oceans are the main home of copepods, though some kinds are found in ponds and lakes. Copepods have one long pair of antennae, a hard case around the body, and feathery legs to help gather food. The largest are about as big as a grape; most are tiny.

COPEPODS
These tiny crustaceans are among the most numerous animals on the planet. They occur in shoals of billions and are the basis of many ocean food chains.

PILL-BUG
This crustacean is an isopod, a member of the woodlouse group. It is one of the few dry-land crustaceans and can roll up into a ball for protection.

More subgroups of crustaceans:

Water-fleas
480 species
- mainly freshwater, a few marine
- small, often transparent
- bob up and down in the water

Fairy and brine shrimps
175 species
- freshwater pools (brine shrimp in salty water)
- feathery legs for swimming and feeding upside down

Copepods
8,400 species
- mainly marine, some freshwater
- long antennae
- swim jerkily

Barnacles
1,000 species
- marine
- adults have shells and live attached to rocks
- some live inside other animals as parasites

INTRODUCTION TO

AMPHIBIANS

The amphibians group includes frogs and toads, newts and salamanders, and the strange, worm-like caecilians. Many seem slow, peaceful creatures. But they are all deadly predators, hunting live prey – from tiny gnats and flies, to rats, snakes and even bats.

A typical amphibian has soft, damp skin and lives in or around water, or in damp places. Like fish, amphibians are cold-blooded animals, which means they take on the temperature of their surroundings. So they are active only in warm conditions. In cold weather they hide in mud or soil, under stones or among damp logs.

TWO LIVES

Although many adult amphibians can live on land, even in deserts, most breed in water. Indeed, the name 'amphibian' means 'two lives', the first part in water and the second on land. The jelly-covered eggs, known as spawn, hatch out as the familiar tadpoles (larvae). These live in water and breathe by gills, before developing lungs, changing shape and growing into adults. This process of changing body shape while growing up is known as metamorphosis.

Amphibians can be found wherever there is fresh water. Most species live in warmer places such as tropical rainforests. Their main defence is to hide, or to rely on the poison glands in their skin.

AMPHIBIANS

FROGS AND TOADS

The distinction between frog and toad is not clear-cut. As a general guide, those with drier, warty, dull-coloured skin and tubby bodies, who tend to walk or waddle, are usually toads. Those with moist skin and slim, brighter-coloured bodies, who leap rather than walk, are usually frogs.

FROG OR TOAD?
The common frogs and toads of Europe fit these descriptions. But elsewhere, especially in the tropics, there is a huge variety of shape and size. Many tropical frogs are brightly coloured, warning that their skin is very poisonous, while others are almost transparent.

The flying frog has broad webbing on its feet, which it uses to glide from tree to tree. Tree frogs are green to match their leafy surroundings and they cling on with their sucker-like toes, hopefully unnoticed. The spadefoot toad uses its powerful rear legs to dig a hole in the ground, where it can hide in safety.

parachute-like webbed toes

MARINE TOAD
Like other amphibians, this toad takes only moving prey, from worms and beetles to flies and fish. If an animal stays still the toad ignores it.

Webbed fingers

FLYING FROG
A glider rather than a true flier, the flying frog of Southeast Asia leaps into mid air to avoid being eaten by a predator. Its body is very thin and light, and its huge hands and feet have parachute-like webs. It can glide up to 50 metres, across a forest clearing or down to the ground or water.

Thin, lightweight legs

Amphibians (Amphibia)
4,000 species
- cold-blooded
- live in water or damp places
- most breed in water
- skin not waterproof
- breathe through skin, gills or lungs

Main groups of amphibians include:

Frogs and toads (Anura)
3,500 species
- jelly-like eggs
- aquatic larvae (tadpoles)
- adults have long hind legs
- most have webbed feet
- no tail when adult

Frog and toad records
- The smallest frogs or toads are less than 2 centimetres long.
- One of the largest is the marine (giant or cane) toad, growing to over 23 centimetres in head-body length.

AMPHIBIANS

SALAMANDERS AND NEWTS

Newts and salamanders have similar lifestyles to frogs and toads. However, their bodies are a different shape, longer and slimmer, with four legs of roughly equal size – and a long tail. They are rarely seen in the wild as they tend to lurk in damp crevices, or hide among water plants. They walk or waddle rather clumsily, but most can swim well with a fish-like bendy motion. Newts have tails which are flattened to give them extra thrust when swimming.

LUNGLESS SALAMANDERS
The largest group of salamanders is the lungless salamanders. They are common in streams and damp woods in parts of North America. As they have no gills or lungs, these amphibians breathe entirely through their skin. So they must keep their

FIRE SALAMANDER
This salamander gets its name from its supposed ability to withstand flames and fire. In fact, when people gathered damp wood for a log fire, the wood sometimes had a salamander hiding in it. This creature soon felt the heat – and seemed to emerge miraculously from the flames.

Bright colours warn that the moist skin is distasteful.

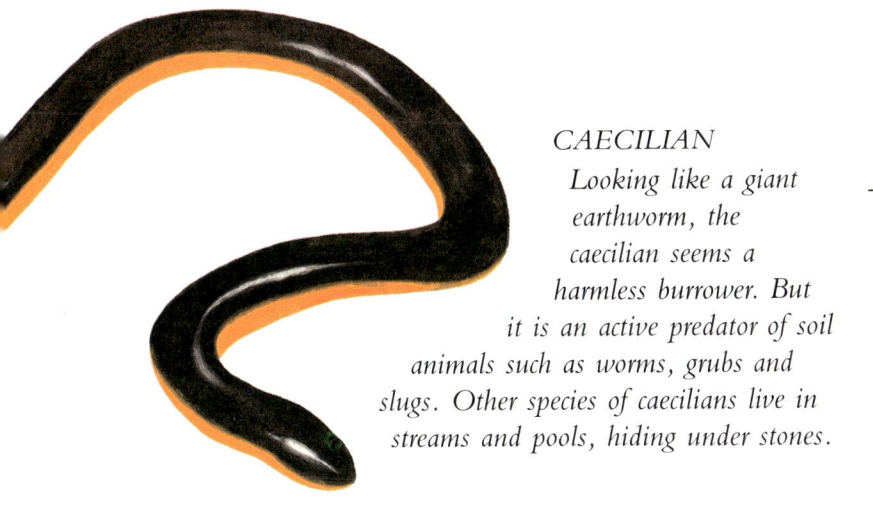

CAECILIAN
Looking like a giant earthworm, the caecilian seems a harmless burrower. But it is an active predator of soil animals such as worms, grubs and slugs. Other species of caecilians live in streams and pools, hiding under stones.

skin damp, which allows oxygen to pass through it. If they dry out, they suffocate and die. Other groups include the burrowing mole-salamanders of North America, the almost legless congo-eels and sirens, and mudpuppies.

MUDPUPPY
An inhabitant of lakes and rivers in eastern North America, this salamander breathes using its feathery gills and eats small fish, water snails, crayfish and freshwater insects.

More groups of amphibians:

Salamanders, newts and mudpuppies (Urodela)
360 species
- long, flexible body
- long tail
- small legs
- larval or tadpole stage (as in frogs and toads)

Caecilians (Apoda)
163 species
- legless
- worm-shaped
- almost blind
- live in damp soil of tropical forests

Biggest amphibian
The largest of all amphibians are the Asian giant salamanders of cold streams in China and Japan. They can grow to more than 150 centimetres in total length and weigh 40 kilograms.

INTRODUCTION TO

REPTILES

Dry, scaly skins characterize the reptiles, which are well adapted to life on land, though some are equally at home in the water. Many reptiles are found in dry habitats such as deserts, but some, notably the turtles, are almost entirely aquatic.

Most reptiles lay eggs. But some lizards and snakes give birth to young or babies, which resemble miniature adults. Even the aquatic reptiles return to dry land to lay their eggs. Reptile eggs are soft and leathery, not hard-shelled like the eggs of birds.

IN COLD BLOOD

Reptiles are cold-blooded and many need to bask in the sun to get warm enough to move quickly. This means there are no reptiles in the coldest parts of the world, on mountain-tops and near the poles.

Lizards and snakes are the most familiar reptiles, but the group also includes turtles and crocodiles, and the strange tuatara. Most reptiles creep, slither or crawl along. A few, however, such as the racerunners and water dragons, can run fast using just their hind legs. Some, such as the basilisk, can even run across the surface of the water.

REPTILES

TURTLES

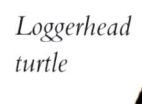

Loggerhead turtle

Turtles, terrapins and tortoises make up the reptile group called the chelonians. Most of the members live either in fresh water or in the sea. The sea turtles are large, and are surprisingly graceful swimmers. The females come ashore on favoured beaches to lay their eggs in pits dug in the sand. The eggs incubate in the heat of the sun and hatch weeks later. The tiny young must race to the sea, usually under cover of darkness, to avoid being eaten by gulls, lizards and other animals who gather for a feast.

FRESHWATER CHELONIANS
Many different kinds of turtles and terrapins are found in rivers, ponds and swamps, mainly in the warmer

MARINE TURTLES
The fully sea-dwelling marine turtles include the leatherback (largest of the group at more than 500 kilograms in weight), loggerhead, hawksbill and Ridley turtles. Most cannot withdraw their head and legs into their shell, and rarely come ashore except to bask in the sun or lay eggs.

Green turtle

Rear legs used for steering

Front legs are powerful flippers for swimming

regions of the world. Many have long, flexible necks to enable them to reach the surface and breathe easily while the rest of the body remains safely submerged. The snapping turtles are fierce predators with powerful jaws. They can catch fish, frogs, young turtles and even small birds. (Tortoises are shown on the next page.)

Reptiles (Reptilia)
6,500 species
- cold-blooded
- dry, scaly skin
- breathe with lungs
- leathery eggs
- no larval stage
- most live on land

Main groups of reptiles include:

Turtles and tortoises (Chelonia)
240 species
- most are aquatic – marine and freshwater
- rounded body encased in hard protective shell
- short, powerful feet, often webbed

FRESHWATER TURTLE
The Murray River turtle is a side-neck, hiding its head in its shell by bending its neck sideways.

49

REPTILES

TORTOISES

Tortoises are land-dwelling members of the turtle group, the chelonians. They are rather slow-moving reptiles, found mainly in warm, dry regions. They use their hard, horny jaws to tear at grasses, fruit and leaves. Although largely vegetarian, tortoises occasionally eat small animals such as insects and slugs.

TORTOISE SHELL
The shell of a tortoise is very hard and forms effective protection against all but the most ingenious of predators. When danger threatens, the tortoise simply pulls in its limbs, head and tail and waits until the coast is clear.

Tortoises were once popular as garden pets, especially in parts of Europe. But they were imported

DESERT TORTOISE
Many tortoises are coloured dull brown or green, to match their surroundings and be camouflaged from predators. The desert tortoise is an excellent digger and excavates a long burrow, where it hides from the intense daytime heat. It emerges in the cool night to feed.

Upper part of shell is carapace

Lower part of shell is plastron

Shell covered with horny plates called scutes

Leopard tortoise

from warmer countries and were not adapted to the cold winters of mid and northern Europe. Wildlife laws now forbid the importing of tortoises in most regions. This saves them from suffering and dying during the cold winter weather.

GIANT TORTOISE
There are several kinds of giant tortoises, each living on an island or group of islands. They eat various types of plant food.

More groups of reptiles:

- **Tortoises (subgroup of Chelonia: Testudinidae)**
  40 species
  - hard shell
  - tough, clawed feet lack the webs of turtles and terrapins
  - live mainly on dry land, even in deserts

- **The biggest tortoises**
  Giant tortoises live on certain isolated islands, especially in the Atlantic and Pacific Oceans.
  - The giant tortoise of the Galapagos Islands in the Pacific grows to about 1.2 metres long and weighs up to 225 kilograms.
  - Even larger is the giant tortoise of the island of Aldabra off East Africa, which can reach 1.8 metres in length.
  - Giant tortoises can live for 150 years or more.

BIG LIZARDS

Most species of lizard are small or medium-sized. However, certain groups contain large species which can be quite impressive – some are even frightening and dangerous to humans.

The iguana group has several large species. One of the most famous is the marine iguana of the Galapagos Islands in the Pacific, off the coast of Ecuador. This species grows to 1.75 metres in length, and as its name suggests, it spends much of its time in the sea, eating seaweeds. It is the only truly marine lizard. It can dive down to 10 metres below the surface and stay submerged for 20 minutes at a time.

Madagascan iguana

Rings of spiny scales on tail

Ear

Long fingers and toes grip well for climbing

THE ORIGINAL DRAGON?

The Komodo dragon is the world's largest lizard. It is a type of monitor lizard and may have given rise to legends about dragons. It can grow to more than three metres long and 100 kilograms in weight. It feeds on other animals, including pigs and small deer.

FRILLED LIZARD
This formidable lizard usually keeps its frill folded against its neck. If threatened, it extends the frill like a multi-coloured fan and hisses loudly with its mouth wide open, to scare away the attacker.

COMMON IGUANA
This American lizard is bright green when young. The bands on the body and tail darken with age.

More subgroups of reptiles:

Lizards (Sauria or Lacertilia)
3,750 species
- Live in most habitats, including deserts, trees, swamps, rivers and the sea
- Most have four slim legs, long tail
- Some lizards, like slow-worms and certain skinks, are legless
- Most are fast and active when warm

Main groups of large lizards:

Iguanas (Iguanidae)
650 species

Monitor lizards (Varanidae)
37 species

Beaded lizards (Helodermatidae)
2 species
- Includes the gila monster and Mexican beaded lizard, the only two lizard species with poisonous bites

SMALLER LIZARDS

Most lizards prefer dry habitats and are active during the day, when the sun warms their bodies. The group with the most species is the skinks. These are rather fat-bodied lizards, often found in sandy habitats. Another large group is the geckos. These are unusual because they hunt during the night. They are mostly found in tropical climates which are warm at night as well as by day. Geckos have very large eyes which help them find their food even in the dusk.

WALKING UP WALLS
Most geckos have another special adaptation. They can run up vertical rocks, walls or even windows and across ceilings. Their toes have ridges with millions of tiny hooks to help them to grip the smoothest surface.

Most lizards have large eyes and good vision

BANDED AGAMA
The bright colours of many lizards are for courtship, to attract a mate at breeding time. The colours also help the lizard to blend in with the bright flowers and plants in its tropical home.

Strong legs for running and climbing

USEFUL SPINES
The thorny devil or moloch is covered in spikes. These protect it from attack and also provide a surface which collects droplets of dew, for the lizard to drink in its Australian desert home.

LEGLESS LIZARDS
Slow-worms are small, legless lizards. In fact they look more like snakes than worms, but unlike a snake, a slow-worm has eyelids.

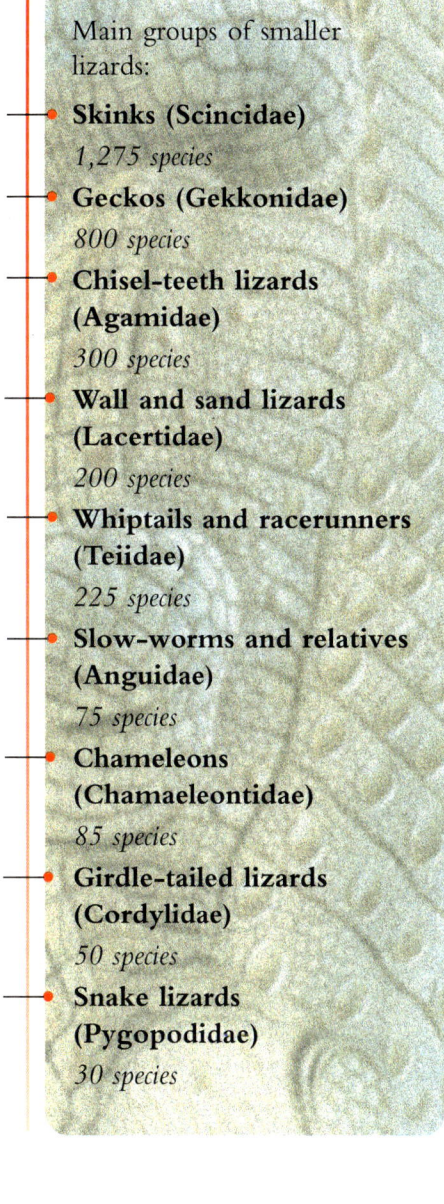

Bright blue tongue

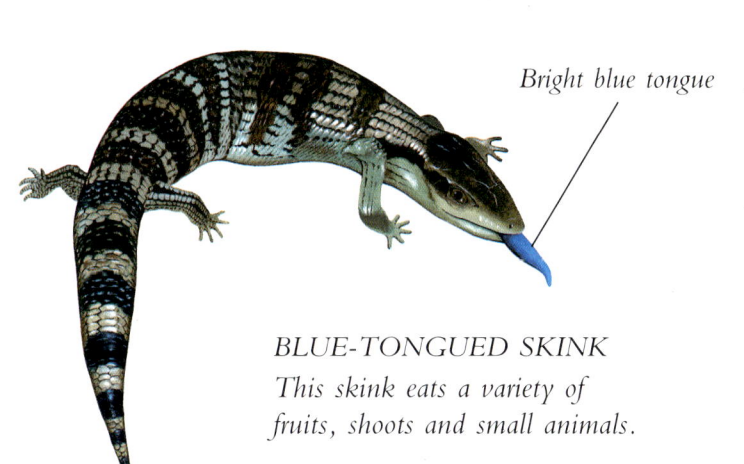

BLUE-TONGUED SKINK
This skink eats a variety of fruits, shoots and small animals.

Main groups of smaller lizards:

Skinks (Scincidae)
1,275 species

Geckos (Gekkonidae)
800 species

Chisel-teeth lizards (Agamidae)
300 species

Wall and sand lizards (Lacertidae)
200 species

Whiptails and racerunners (Teiidae)
225 species

Slow-worms and relatives (Anguidae)
75 species

Chameleons (Chamaeleontidae)
85 species

Girdle-tailed lizards (Cordylidae)
50 species

Snake lizards (Pygopodidae)
30 species

REPTILES

Non-Poisonous Snakes

PYTHON
The reticulated python, from Southeast Asia, can kill mammals as large as a pig or a small deer using the constrictor method.

Body thrown into S-curves as snake slithers

Although we may think of snakes as dangerous and unpleasant, in fact only about one-fifth of all snake species are poisonous. And only about a hundred of these are aggressive enough, with teeth strong enough, and venom powerful enough, to harm people.

SQUEEZED TO DEATH
Nevertheless, some of the larger non-poisonous snakes sometimes pose a threat – particularly those which kill their prey by suffocation, such as the larger pythons and boas. These snakes are called constrictors. They wrap their muscular bodies around their prey and slowly squeeze it to

ANACONDA
The largest snakes are the reticulated python of Southeast Asia and the anaconda of South America, which may reach 10 metres in length. The amethystine python is Australia's largest snake; it can grow as long as seven metres.

Neck and gullet are elastic to stretch for swallowing large victims

Eyes lack eyelids, giving snakes a 'glassy' stare

Large scales on underside tilt to grip the ground

death, before devouring it whole. Each time the victim tries to breathe, the snake grips tighter until breathing becomes impossible. After a large meal, these snakes rest for weeks as they digest the victim. Pythons often rest coiled in tree branches.

Another reptile subgroup:

- **Snakes (Serpentes or Ophidia)**
2,400 species
  - long, narrow body
  - no legs
  - no eyelids
  - no eardrums
  - all snakes hunt prey, a few specialize on scavenging or items such as eggs

The main (mostly non-poisonous) snake groups include:

- **Typical snakes (Colubridae)**
1,500 species
- **Blind snakes (Typhlopidae)**
160 species
- **Boas (Boidae)**
40 species
- **Pythons (Pythonidae)**
30 species

REPTILES

POISONOUS SNAKES

Poisonous snakes use their long teeth or fangs to inject venom into their prey when they bite. Although some snakes are aggressive, most people get bitten when they tread on a poisonous snake by accident, and the snake strikes back in self-defence. Snake bites still kill thousands of people each year, although anti-venoms are now usually available for treatment.

Hood spread to reveal eyespots

FRONT-FANGED SNAKES

Some of the most dangerous snakes, such as cobras, mambas and the taipan of Australia, belong to the front-fanged snake family. Although their fangs are not as efficient at delivering venom as those of the other main group, the vipers, the cobras and coral

CAPE COBRA
Cobras can extend the loose ribs on either side of the head and neck, to form a hood-like flap of skin. This warns that the snake is ready to strike. It also raises itself off the ground to get a clearer view and easier aim. The king cobra preys mainly on other snakes and also lizards. The female Indian cobra is unusual among snakes since she guards her eggs until they hatch.

Flicking tongue detects airborne scents

TAIPAN
This sleek, fast, rapid-striking snake lives in north-east Australia and New Guinea.

snakes often hang onto their victim and make chewing movements to increase the flow of poison. The sea snakes include some of the world's most venomous species. Although sea snakes have highly toxic venom, they are not usually aggressive and tend not to inject much venom when they do bite.

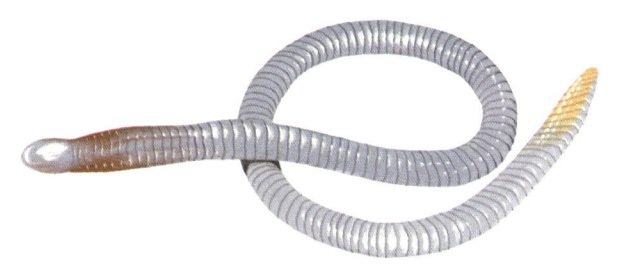

WORM-LIZARDS
These reptiles have their own subgroup, the amphisbaenids. They look like large earthworms and burrow in the soils of tropical forests, hunting small animals.

Groups of poisonous snakes:

Front-fanged snakes (Elapidae)
240 species
- includes death adder, cobras, mambas, taipan, kraits, coral snakes, tiger snakes and sea snakes

Vipers (Viperidae)
190 species
- includes adders, vipers, cottonmouth, fer-de-lance, bushmaster, copperhead, rattlesnakes, sidewinder

- Spitting cobras from Africa and Southeast Asia sometimes spray venom into the eyes of a victim.
- The largest poisonous snake is the king cobra, over five metres in length.
- The most dangerous is probably the Indian cobra which kills thousands of people each year. The snakes with the deadliest venom are the black mamba of Africa and the taipan of Australia.

REPTILES

CROCODILES

Crocodiles, alligators, caimans and gharials form the crocodilian group of reptiles. They are the largest of all the reptiles, and also the most similar to their ancient cousins the dinosaurs, with their heavy skin and powerful jaws. Their jaws are very muscular and can clamp shut with huge force. They are lined with sharp teeth with which they can easily tear the flesh of their prey – mainly fish, mammals and water birds. The gharial is a specialist fish-eater from Asia. It has a more delicate, thinner snout.

HUNTING METHODS
Most crocodilians lie in wait for their prey, almost submerged. Then, when the prey is within range they surge

ESTUARINE CROCODILE
This huge reptile an be found in the open sea as well as in rivers and estuaries. It is a powerful swimmer, and large and strong enough to overcome most victims, from deer to sea turtles and large fish. Because of persecution and hunting, it is now rare, and is protected by law in most regions.

Eyes on top of head

Nile crocodile

forward and drag it under water, holding it down until it drowns. One of the strangest things about crocodiles and alligators is that they cover their eggs with rotting compost. This keeps the eggs warm, so that they can incubate and the babies develop inside.

Flattened tail for swimming

CAREFUL MOTHER
The mother crocodile guards her eggs until they hatch. The babies make squeaking noises and she carries them carefully to the water in her mouth.

The crocodilian group of reptiles has three main subgroups:

Crocodiles (Crocodylidae)
14 species

Alligators and caimans (Alligatoridae)
7 species

Gharial (Gavialidae)
1 species

Largest reptiles
These are the estuarine or saltwater crocodiles of Southern Asia and Northern Australia.
- These giants can reach over 7.5 metres in length.
- They feed mainly on fish and crustaceans, but will also take other vertebrates, and can be a danger to people.

INDEX

A
abdomen 22, 23, 24, 25, 33,
amphibian 40-45
animals: cold-blooded, 40, 43, 47, 49
ant 25
antennae 22, 26, 30, 37, 38, 39
ant-lion 27
aphid 26, 27,
arachnid 8, 32-35
arthropod 8, 9, 18, 32-37

B
baby 46, 61
backbone 8
barnacle 36, 39
basilisk 47
bat 40
bee 24-25
beetle 22, 23, 26-27, 42
bird 26, 33, 46, 49, 60; gull 48
bivalve 19
breeding 22, 43, 44
brine shrimp 39
brittle-star 20, 21
bug 26, 26-27
  leaf 26; water 26
bumblebee, 25

butterfly
  blue 9; brimstone 23; tropical blue 22

C
caecilian, 40, 41, 45
camouflage 30
carnivore 35
caterpillar 23
cell 10, 12
centipede 35
chrysalis 23
cicada 26, 27
cilia 11
claw 11
cnidarian 12-13
cocoon 32
coelenterates 12-13
comb jelly 13
congo-eel 45
copepod 39
coral 12, 13, 21
crab 8, 36-37, 38
  shore crab 36; spider crab 36
crayfish 36, 37, 45
cricket 30-31
crustacean, 8, 36-39, 61
ctenophore 13
cuttlefish 19

D
damselfly 28, 29

deer 53, 60
desert 41, 46, 51, 53
dragonfly 28-29

E
earwig 28, 29
echinoderm 20-21
egg 17, 23, 24, 31, 32, 35, 38, 41, 43, 46, 48, 49, 61

F
fairy shrimp 38, 39
feather-star 20, 21
fish 12, 28, 36, 38, 40, 42, 44, 45, 49, 60, 61
fly 24-25, 40, 42
  bluebottle 24; cranefly 24; dungfly 24; fruitfly 24; gnat 24, 28, 40; horsefly 24; housefly 24; hoverfly 24; midge 24; mosquito 24
frog 40, 42-43, 44, 45, 49
flying 42, 43; red-eyed tree frog 41; tree frog 42

G
gecko 54
gharial 60, 61
grasshopper 30-31,

grub 28, 45

H
habitat 16, 17, 33, 36, 46, 53, 54
harvestman 32, 33
hemipteran 26
herbivore 35
honeybee 25
hopper 26
hydra 13
Hymenoptera 25

I
iguana 52, 53; common, 53; Madagascan 52; Marine, 52
imago 23
insect 8, 15, 22-31, 45, 50; life cycle of 23; social 25
intestine 17
invertebrate 8-39
isopod 39

J
jellyfish 9, 12-13
  Aurelia 8; Moon 12

K
katydid 30

L
lacewing 8, 27
ladybird 26
larva 15, 23, 25, 27, 28, 31, 41, 43, 45, 49
leaf insect 31
leech 15
lemur 154-55
lizard 46, 47, 48, 52-55; banded agama 46, 54; beaded 53; frilled 53; Komodo dragon 53; monitor 53; skink 53, 54; slow-worm 53, 54; thorny devil 55
lobster 36, 37
locust 30
louse 26, 27

M
maggot 25
mammal 26, 33, 34, 60
man-o-war 13
mantis 29; praying 29
mate 22, 27, 30, 31, 54
mayfly 28, 31
metamorphosis 23, 41
millipede 35
mite 32-33
mollusc 9, 15, 18-19
moss animal 11
moth 22, 23
mudpuppy 45
mussel 18, 95, 194

N
nectar 23
newt 40, 44-45; crested 40; Nile monitor 47
nymph 28, 29, 31

O
octopus 18, 19
oyster 18, 95

P
parapodia 14
parasite 15, 16, 17, 26, 27, 33, 39
phylum 8
pig 17
pill-bug 39
plant 44, 51, 54; water, 44
prawn 8, 12, 36-37, 38
pupa 23

R
racerunner 47
rainforest 41
rat 40
reproduction 17
reptile 33, 46-61; alligator 46, 60, 61; crocodile 47, 60-61; estuarine 60; Nile 61
rotifer 11

S
salamander 40, 44-45; Asian giant 45; fire 41, 44; mole-salamander 45
sand dollar 20, 21
scorpion 32, 34, 35
sea anemone 12, 13
sea cucumber 20, 21,
sea lily 20, 21
sea urchin 20-21
seaweed 52
shell 9
shellfish 18, 20
shrimp 8, 12, 36, 37
siren 45
skeleton 9, 11, 12, 13
slug 18, 19, 45, 50
snail 9, 18, 19; common (garden) 9, 18
snake 40, 46, 47, 55, 56-59; anaconda, 57; blind 57; boa 57; cobra 47, 58; constrictors 56-57; coral 58-59; Indian cobra 59; king cobra 59; mamba 58; python 56, 57; sea snakes 59; taipan 58, 59; typical 57; viper 58
soil 14, 16, 28, 35, 40, 45, 59
spawn 41
spider 8, 29, 32-33; bird-eating 33; sun spider 9, 34; trapdoor 32-33
sponge, 10, 11
starfish 20-21, 20
stick insect 31
squid 18, 19

T
tadpole 28, 41, 43, 45
tentacle 11, 12, 13, 18, 19, 21
termite 25
terrapin 48, 51
thorax 22, 23, 24
tick 32, 33
toad 40, 42-43, 44, 45, marine 40, 42; spade foot 42
tortoise 48, 49, 50-51; desert 50; giant 51; Leopard 51
tuatara 47
turtle 46, 47, 48-51; green 47, 48; loggerhead 49; marine 48; Murray River 49; sea 48, 60; snapping 49

V
vegetarian 50
vertebrate 8, 61

W
wasp 24-25
water-bear 10, 11
water dragon 47
water-flea 36, 38, 39
weevil 26, 27
woodlouse 36, 38, 39
worm 9, 12, 14-17, 42, 45, 55; bristleworm 14, 15; earthworm 14, 15, 16, 45, 59, 121; flatworm 16, 17; lugworm 14, 15; nematode 16, 17; ribbon 17; ragworm 16, 17; roundworm 16, 17; segmented 14, 15; tapeworm 17
worm-lizard 59

63

ACKNOWLEDGEMENTS

The publishers wish to thank the following artists who have contributed to this book.

David Ashby, Mike Atkinson, Wayne Ford, Roger Kent, Stuart Lafford (Linden Artists), Alan Male (Linden Artists), Terry Riley.

All photographs from the Miles Kelly Archive.